MW01385149

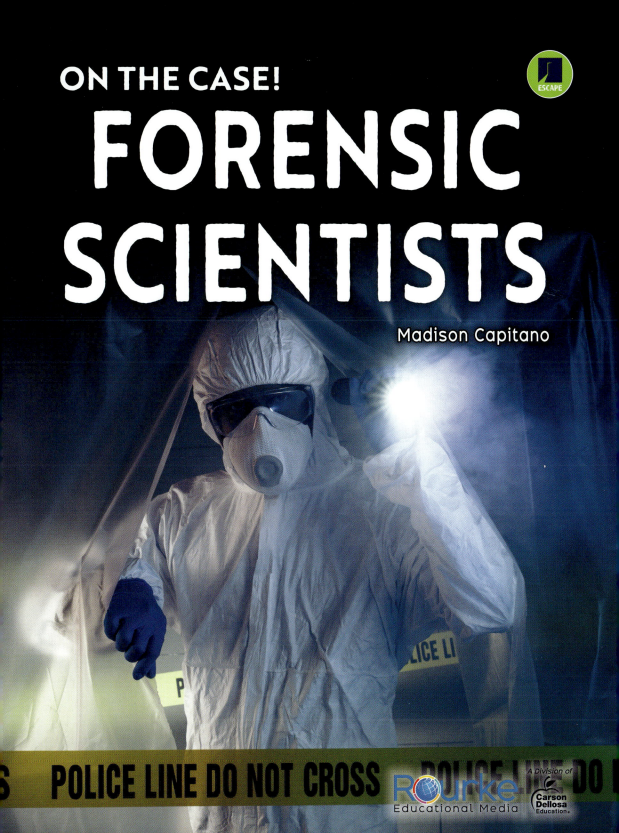

ON THE CASE!

FORENSIC SCIENTISTS

Madison Capitano

POLICE LINE DO NOT CROSS

Rourke
Educational Media

A Division of
Carson
Dellosa
Education

BEFORE AND DURING READING ACTIVITIES

Before Reading: *Building Background Knowledge and Vocabulary*

Building background knowledge can help children process new information and build upon what they already know. Before reading a book, it is important to tap into what children already know about the topic. This will help them develop their vocabulary and increase their reading comprehension.

Questions and Activities to Build Background Knowledge:

1. Look at the front cover of the book and read the title. What do you think this book will be about?
2. What do you already know about this topic?
3. Take a book walk and skim the pages. Look at the table of contents, photographs, captions, and bold words. Did these text features give you any information or predictions about what you will read in this book?

Vocabulary: *Vocabulary Is Key to Reading Comprehension*

Use the following directions to prompt a conversation about each word.

- Read the vocabulary words.
- What comes to mind when you see each word?
- What do you think each word means?

Vocabulary Words:
- contaminate
- fibers
- forensic
- latent
- suspects
- tissue

During Reading: *Reading for Meaning and Understanding*

To achieve deep comprehension of a book, children are encouraged to use close reading strategies. During reading, it is important to have children stop and make connections. These connections result in deeper analysis and understanding of a book.

 Close Reading a Text

During reading, have children stop and talk about the following:

- Any confusing parts
- Any unknown words
- Text to text, text to self, text to world connections
- The main idea in each chapter or heading

Encourage children to use context clues to determine the meaning of any unknown words. These strategies will help children learn to analyze the text more thoroughly as they read.

When you are finished reading this book, turn to the next-to-last page for After Reading Questions and an Activity.

TABLE OF CONTENTS

ON THE CASE

Evidence can be the key to solving a crime. **Forensic** scientists are the professionals responsible for understanding the evidence in criminal investigations. They gather evidence, test evidence, and provide expert knowledge about what it means!

» **forensic** (fuh-REN-sik): using science and technology to investigate evidence and establish facts

4

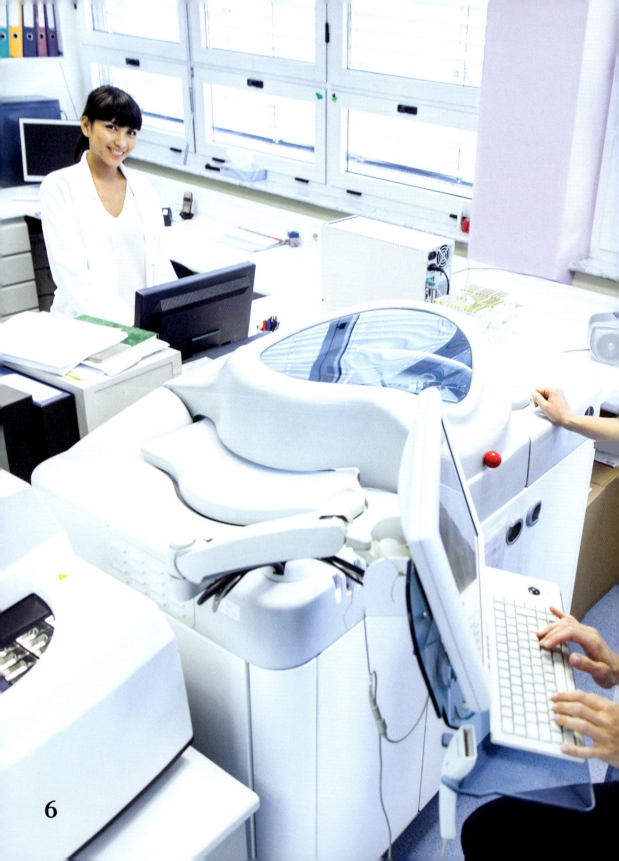

There are many different kinds of forensic scientists. Chemicals, DNA, plants, teeth, and weapons are all subjects they can study. They all use their skills to help solve crimes.

BAG AND TAG

Detectives arrive at a crime scene, but it is a complete mess! A type of forensic scientist called a crime scene investigator is on the case.

8

Forensic scientists look for all kinds of evidence. Biological evidence can be blood, **tissue**, or hair. Trace evidence includes **fibers**, soil, and small pieces of glass or bullets.

» **tissue** (TISH-oo): biological evidence, such as skin or flesh, that must be preserved for forensic analysis

» **fibers** (FYE-burs): thin strands of material that can be used to forensically match things such as clothing, carpets, or cars

11

Crime scene investigators carefully put evidence in bags. They label each bag and write a report. Their work uncovered a tiny drop of blood that helped solve the case!

STEP ONE

If crime scene investigators do not wear protective gear, they could **contaminate** evidence. To stop this, they wear plastic suits, slippers, gloves, and hairnets.

» **contaminate** (kuhn-TAM-uh-nayt): to soil, stain, corrupt, or infect by touching something or letting it come into contact with something else

13

HIDDEN CLUES

When a crime scene shows no fingerprints, detectives are worried they won't catch the criminal. But, there's more than meets the eye. Forensic scientists are on the case!

WHAT IS A PRINT?

Fingerprints are made up of whorls, loops, ridges, and arches. These patterns combine to make a print that is unique. The first fingerprint evidence used in the United States was over 100 years ago!

15

Every fingerprint is unique. When someone's fingerprint is found at a crime scene, investigators can be sure that person was there.

A forensic scientist collects fingerprints. They do this in several different ways. One way is by using a special powder. They dust the powder over surfaces to reveal prints.

Another way to collect fingerprints is with cyanoacrylate, also called super glue! It is used to find **latent** fingerprints on surfaces such as glass, plastic, and metal. The cyanoacrylate is turned into a gas. The gas is sprayed on surfaces scientists think might have fingerprints. The prints come into view like magic.

» **latent** (LAY-tuhnt): present, but not yet active or visible

18

Fuming chambers seal in the cyanoacrylate vapors to reveal fingerprints.

19

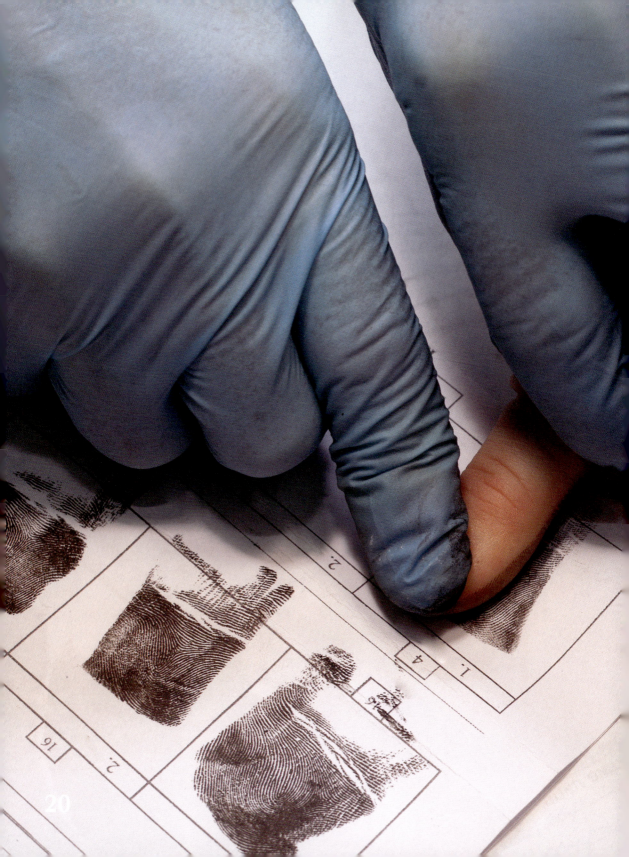

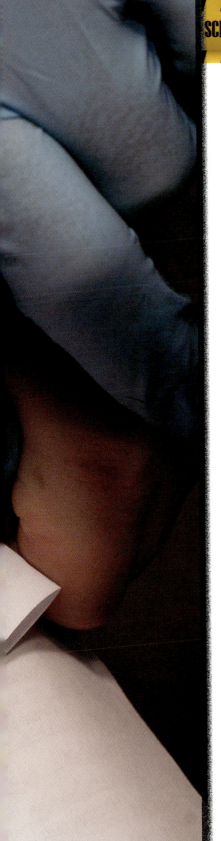

Forensic scientists used cyanoacrylate on evidence from the crime scene. They found a latent print on a tea kettle! They can now use computer databases to match this print with possible **suspects**.

» **suspects** (SUHS-pekts): people who are thought to have committed a crime

BUGGING OUT

A woman has been in jail for years for a murder. But her lawyer says she could not have been there at the time of the crime. Believe it or not, bugs could hold the answers. A type of forensic scientist called a forensic entomologist is on the case!

CREEPY CRAWLY

Entomology is the study of insects. A forensic entomologist usually studies insects on dead bodies.

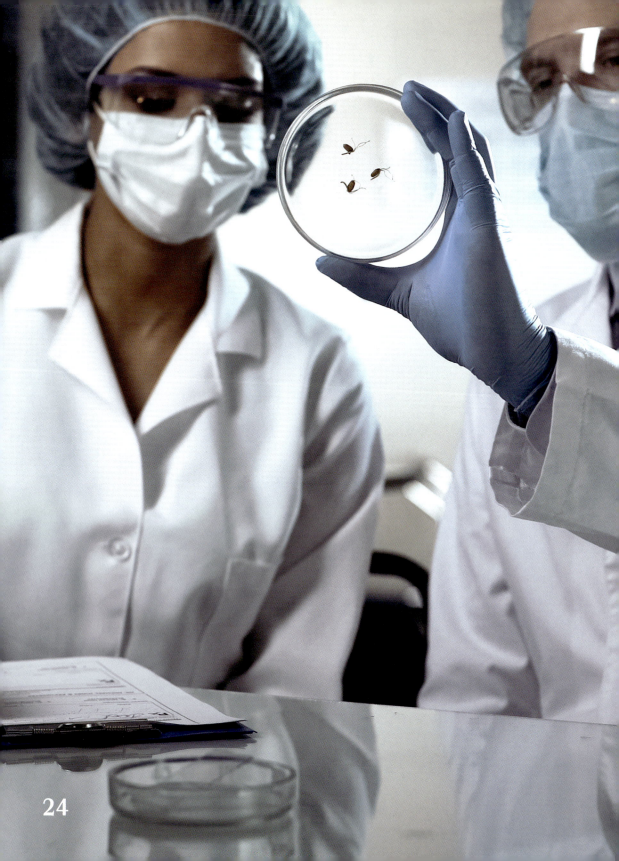

Blowflies can provide lots of clues. They have a specific life cycle. They live only during certain seasons. They like warm temperatures. Finally, they are active during the day and they rest at night.

THE BLOWFLY LIFE CYCLE

Day 0: A dead body attracts insects such as the blowfly. A blowfly can lay around 300 eggs on the body, usually near an open wound.

Day 1: The eggs hatch into larvae, also called maggots, and start feeding.

Day 2: The larvae molt, or shed their skin.

Day 3: They molt again and continue to feed.

Day 5: The maggots leave the body.

Day 9: They complete their transformation into adult blowflies.

25

Reports showed that the body had no blowflies. Forensic entomologists used this evidence to prove that the crime happened after dark. The woman's lawyer showed that she was somewhere else that night. After years in prison, blowflies and forensic science proved a woman innocent!

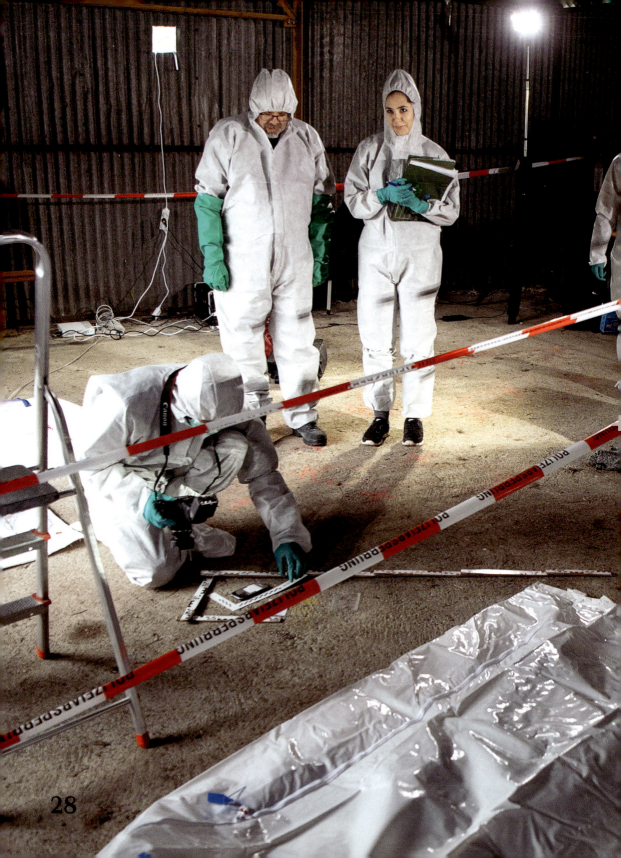

Forensic scientists work hard to find evidence. They use science to understand what the evidence means. When criminals leave behind questions, forensic scientists are on the case!

MEMORY GAME

Look at the pictures. What do you remember reading on the pages where each image appeared?

INDEX

AFTER READING QUESTIONS

1. What do crime scene investigators wear when they collect evidence?

2. What do you think is the most interesting part of a forensic scientist's job?

3. What are two patterns that can be part of a fingerprint?

4. How many eggs can blowflies lay at one time?

5. Would you like to be a forensic scientist? Why or why not?

ACTIVITY

Using a marker or highlighter, color the tip of your finger. Then, press a clear piece of tape over your finger while the ink is wet. Gently remove the tape and stick it on a sheet of white paper to see your fingerprint! What patterns can you see? Are the prints on your other fingers different? How?

ABOUT THE AUTHOR

Madison Capitano is a writer in Columbus, Ohio, who loves to watch mystery shows! She's not a scientist, but she loves how forensic scientists work to find missing information. Madison used to read books to her little brother and sister all the time. Now she loves to write books for other kids to enjoy.

www.rourkeeducationalmedia.com

PHOTO CREDITS: page 1: ©D-Keine / iStock; page 5: ©microgen / iStock; page 6: ©choja / iStock; page 9: ©jpgfactory / iStock; page 10: ©D-Keine / iStock; page 13: ©digicomphoto / iStock; page 15: ©living_images / iStock; page 16: ©zoka74 / iStock; page 19: ©Anthony Nelson / U.S Air Force; page 20: ©franz12 / iStock; page 23: ©AaronAmat / iStock; page 24: ©Motortion Films / Shutterstock; page 27: ©AZemdega / iStock; page 28: ©Sebastian Gollnow/dpa/picture-alliance/Newscom / Newscom; caution tape: ©tcenitelkrasoti / Pixabay; magnifying glass: ©Pixaline / Pixabay

Edited by: Kim Thompson
Cover design by: Kathy Walsh
Interior design by: Sara Radka

Library of Congress PCN Data

Forensic Scientists / Madison Capitano
(On the Case!)
   ISBN 978-1-73163-817-5 (hard cover)
   ISBN 978-1-73163-894-6 (soft cover)
   ISBN 978-1-73163-971-4 (e-Book)
   ISBN 978-1-73164-048-2 (e-Pub)
Library of Congress Control Number: 2020930273

Rourke Educational Media
Printed in the United States of America
01-1942011937